Lung Lost

J.M. Marie

Published by J.M. Marie, 2024.

To the man who knows the story behind every scar.

FOREWORD

The first time I met J.M. Marie was in the smoking section of a grungy little restaurant mall. She lit up the room when she walked in; a shining soul that could blind the very gods. One of the first things we discussed was a tattoo she had and how badly she wanted to cover it up. She thought it was awful. I thought *she* was awesome. We connected pretty instantly, and I had a feeling I'd be seeing more of her.

†

I was right.

†

J.M. feels things very deeply, and that was something I could relate to. I'd even go so far as to say she feels what other people are feeling, too. As you read through this book, you'll see what I mean. It's an intimate portrait of love, loss, betrayal, abuse, and internal conflict, leading to the author finally finding peace within. As you take this journey with her, remember that life is often a mess of misconceptions and confusion. It's not just good, and it's not just bad. But things do get better if you do the work and get to know who you really are. No one else can decide that for you.

†

This is the first book I've edited in a while, and I was both thrilled and humbled that Marie asked me to write this foreword. As a fellow poet and author, it brings me so much joy to help others realize their writing dreams. I think she has a long, fulfilling, creative path to follow.

†

In this book, I hope you will see a mirror. In the reflection, I hope you find that you are never alone. Every woman who ever struggled like this is beside you, including J.M. Marie and I.

†

Journey on, my friends, and rise up.

INTRODUCTION

All of our journeys are unique and my story may not look like yours. On the other hand, it may resemble yours more than either of us would like. Underneath all our Survivor stories there is pain, loss, and hope. That is why I am sharing this part of mine with you; I have more I could tell. I have decades of trauma, heartache, joy and love. I wanted to start with a turning point. I wanted to start with a comeback. I'm not where I want to be, but I'm far from where I've been and I know I'm strong enough to get there. You are too!

†

Women need to support other women. To get each other through. I may not know you, but I want you to get through it. I want you to do what it takes to claw and fight and rise. I want you to seize your happiness in the world.

†

I have included in the back of this book some resources if you need help getting there. I also want you to know I am here for you. You can reach out to me on Instagram or my Facebook page. You aren't alone. We are in this together.

†

J.M. Marie

1 THE DEVIL YOU KNOW

After so many years
And the tears that you cry
When you're all alone
Night after night

†

Now it's the last straw
You're gonna leave him this time
You're out the door
Disappear out of sight

†

Give all your trust
Put your heart on the line
Just to get crushed and
Drown in a bottle of wine

†

Better stick to the devil you know
Darlin'
Than to watch it all go

†

Leavin' your home
Pack your stuff and say goodbye
You fall and eat dirt
Taste those tears that you cry

†

You choke down your fears
Make the decision to try
Just to turn back around
And let that chance slip on by

†

You promised forever and
After all, he's sorry
It's not always like this
Tell your friends not to worry

†

Your fear is a cage
Casting doubt in your mind
'Cos with freedom comes hope
And you can't take the grind

†

Yeah, the devil you know
Darlin'
Beats the love that you don't

21

I took all my clothes off
And I asked him how I looked
"Like a Goddess"
He said

3 II

I don't just walk on eggshells; they're razor-blades and I have to
walk so lightly
because they'll scream like an alarm
Blow like a landmine
Explode like a nuke
And it'll take everything I have to hold onto the Earth

†

Sometimes I shake and rage when I'm backed into a corner and
shoved against the wall
Then, sometimes,
Wail, like a sad, sorrowful siren into the night

†

You come home from work. Pick a fight.
Wake up in the morning. Pick a fight.
There's an ache in me
Intangible, but ever-present, and so very real
So, let's just get to the heart of it
Ask the question;
Why treat me like this?

†

Bound by humility
Trapped underneath the stairs

Silence used to cut through my heart like glass
But now I soak in it, wishing I could absorb it for use later.

4 THAT'S LOVING YOU

Almost forgot what it felt like
To be held like this
Adored so completely
Soaking in this bliss
You came in as I was pushing the world out
Pressed my body up against the door
Couldn't stop you from breaking it down
Don't know what I was even fighting it for

†

Cos you make me smile when I wanna cry
You think I'm worth fighting for
I don't even know why
Your touch calms my demons
Your love sets me free
Your kisses are fire
And they consume all of me

5 III

Happiness doesn't come easy for me
And when it does, it's often ripped away quickly
So, I sip it slowly
Hold it in my mouth
Let it slide over my taste buds and try to burn it into my memories
So, I won't ever forget this feeling
When the cold, dark, hopelessness creeps back in.

6 RAIN MIXING WITH HOT TEARS

What even *is* love? What is this feeling we all want
That causes so much pain and joy? So much bliss and sorrow?
Yet, nobody can define it.

†

I didn't know a soul could hurt...but mine does.
I didn't know I even had a soul.
I didn't know.

†

I think this is the price I have to pay for what we had.
It burned so brilliant and white hot
And now this is the pain that follows. Lingering, tender,
forever

†

I was so lucky to have you.
People spend their lives searching and chasing what I feel for
you
Most will never find it
I was so lucky to love and be loved by you

7 BIRD

I will never again be controlled or manipulated.
I won't allow you to bury my suffering under your own
To make it all about you
I matter
I am the heart, the guts *and* the backbone of this family
I deserve to be happy
I deserve to experience joy and pleasure.
I deserve love and tenderness and intimacy and passion

†

You don't get to take any more from me
You've taken enough
And I've given enough
That's over.
Your era of double standards and hypocrisy is over

†

The cracked shell that I was is breaking apart
And I will never be caged again

8 MY UNBREAKING

I didn't ask you to save me
I didn't know the words to beg you to stay
I couldn't get the sounds past my throat
But you knew, and you did.

†

I didn't know about you
When I was a little girl and learning how rough the world is.
I didn't know during the worst years there was someone out there
Who would find me, wipe away my tears and cover my bruises with kisses
I didn't know you existed.
"Fairy tales," I said, "That's all that is."

†

I didn't know I could be fixed.
I didn't know it wouldn't always be like this.
I didn't know you would take control
I didn't know you'd give me everything I need
And then
I didn't know you were going to put a crown on my head and a sword in my hand and order me to save myself.

9 IV

What was it all for, just to end up like this?
What's the lesson?
Where is the silver lining?

†

I believed you
So, I let you in
Now I wish to God that we never fucking met
Was every part of it a lie?
The flame you ignited inside me?
The tender look in your eyes?
The way you held me?
Was any of it real?

10 V

You told me to run
You told me with your devil eyes
And the wicked things you'd say
You told me with your games and lies
You warned me not to stay

†

You told me to run
With your mood swings
Your short fuse
Your inability to accept accountability

†

You told me to run
Every time we didn't see eye to eye
Every time reality became too hard to ignore
But I didn't listen, I just continued to stay and try

†

Had me questioning myself
Had me doubting everything
You wanted me broken and damaged
So, I should have run

11 VI

Can you hear me?
Can you hear me screaming in my head?
Can you hear me screaming, "I love you"
"Don't go"
"Stay forever"

†

Sometimes I think you can hear it
The words I can't say
The sounds I can't get past my throat
You look at me like you know
Like you hear my soul crying out for you

†

And I can hear you.
I can feel you.
I can feel your soul telling mine it's going to be OK.
I see love in your eyes
And I can hear in your breathing
That you're settling in for the long haul

†

Your arms around me again
And your lips touch my neck
I'm home.

12 VII

I'll always be someone watching others walk away
I'll always be here replaying everything I said and did
Trying to piece together what I did wrong

†

Sometimes it's a lot
Sometimes I really don't even know
But here I stand while you move on
I'm so easy to replace
I'm so easy to erase
I'm so hard to love
I'm so hard to relate to
I'm so hard to make sense of
I'm so hard to forgive
I bet the next one won't be so hard.

13 THE CRUELEST TRICK THE DEVIL EVER PLAYED

You cried inside of me
And I pulled away

†

Our slice of heaven.
Our moment in time.
The sunset came so soon
I can still hear you
I can still taste you on my lips
I still feel your touch
I hear your heart beating
And when I close my eyes my head is on your chest again

†

But it's not real
It'll never be real
It'll never be us
It'll never be right

†

It was a beautiful illusion
Sweet lies

Stolen time
Electric chemistry
Passion and tenderness
That I'll remember for all of forever

14 BROKEN TOY

I knew before you even left the hotel that something had changed
I feel like such a fool
For having believed you
For soaking up every word
Like it was gospel that would save me and my soul

†

You scaled my walls
And you convinced my skeptical heart
That I could trust you
And that you loved me.
And then you left me in the rain
With my tear soaked cheeks
And every bit of me shattered on the ground

†

So go ahead and find a problem.
Pick a fight
Find some way to make this about me
And not that you just got what you wanted from me
And you're done playing
After all, no one likes a broken toy

15 VIII

I'm so angry because I *knew*
I knew what you were
I had all these doubts
I didn't trust you
But somehow you got in
You manipulated me
You made me fall for your lies
And I opened up to you
That's the worst part
I bared my very soul to you
And you drank it all in
And left me empty and weak
You siphoned my love and left me with nothing but a broken
heart
And the inability to trust even myself
You always said you'd destroy me
You did

16 EXCEPT FOR WHEN YOU PUT A DAGGER IN MY HEART AND TWISTED

When I told you to hurt me I didn't mean my heart
Now there's blood everywhere
But it never lands on you, does it?

†

I shouldn't have to prove myself to you
Over and over and over again
So, why do I feel like I do?
You said you'd break me
And I guess I didn't understand

†

I expected bruises, bloodshed, maybe broken bones
To be hollowed out so completely that maybe, just maybe
Everything rotten in me would fall out like a decayed pumpkin
But I underestimated you
I never saw this coming
I never expected you'd both break my heart and steal my soul
Take everything from me and make me watch you leave
With such indifference

†

It would almost hurt less if you just told me how worthless you
think I am
and how you thought I'd be a fun game
But that I'm not even as much fun as you thought
Except for when you put a dagger in my heart and twisted

17 IX

Maybe I'll watch the sunrise
I hear they're worth seeing
Watch the darkness fade to new beginnings
The light intensify into what comes next
Maybe it won't be so bad after that
Maybe it'll drive out the darkness in me too
Or even just hurt a little bit less.

18 X

It clutches my heart with a steel grip and claws
It fills my chest with a violent dread
My throat closes up and I can't breathe
Can't speak
Can't dream
Fear comes over my entire being
The urge to run, and the inexplicable *knowing*
That there is nowhere I can ever run that will be safe
I can't hide from it anywhere
Perpetual tears behind my eyes threaten
And it takes all I have to hold them back
This lump in my throat has become my only constant
If it were ever to leave me what would I say?
Would the breaths come easier?
Would I be able to say the right things?
Or would I make it even worse?

†

So I am
Alone in my sorrow, my fear, my dread, my anger, my pain
And everything else that makes me the way I am
So fucking unlovable

19 XI

If I can't scream to the sky
I'll fall to my knees in despair
If I can't rage at every sunrise
And moan to the sunset
I'll curl up in the shower and sob

†

Someday they won't know I existed
But maybe my words will remain somewhere
And if I can't have you
Maybe I can find peace someday in silence and disdain

20 SOMEWHERE, IT'S YOU

Do you ever stop to think about us, other places?
About us in alternate realities?
Cos I do
I think about the versions of us that are together
The versions of us that got it right.

†

Somewhere, right now, you are waking up and making coffee
I'm stretching out in bed
Naked and happy from a night of passion
From a night of you ripping orgasm after orgasm out of me
And kissing me deeply
And holding me tenderly

†

Somewhere, you and I are dancing in the rain
We aren't fighting
You aren't leaving me
I'm not crying in a fit of panic
Or howling my despair at the moon
We are dancing
And we are in love

†

Somewhere, it's you I belong with
Somewhere, it's you I belong to
And you belong to me, too

21 XII

When August yearnings
Stolen kisses and hungry touches
Turn to September lies under midnight skies
My October dreams and their loosely stitched seams
Because, deep down I never really believed you anyway
But, God damn, I wanted to.
November brings the slow death
Bury the body before the ground freezes

22 XIII

The calm before the storm is anxious energy
But the calm that comes after is so melancholy
That maybe I'll sleep tonight

23 XIV

I'll stand again
I won't do it with grace
I'll wince and my movements will be slow
Battle worn and bruised
But I will stand again

†

I'll love again
I'll do it cautiously
The walls you tore down, I will build stronger and taller
They will have to work harder than you did
To get to my tender heart
But I will love again

†

I'll cry again
It won't be like this though.
It will be for a moment
Moments of joy, moments of anger, moments of grief
Yea, I'll cry again
But only for a little while.

24 XV

There's no forever left in the whole world
Promises are just plans made with kind intention
With no follow through
Sometimes pretty words are just pretty words
Who are you without them?
If your actions were to define you, could I trust you?
Or do you lie with your movements?

†

Nothing is endless
Except possibilities
That's why my heart is such a dreamer
And my brain takes the reins
"Get a hold of yourself, you fool!
Don't you remember the times before?
Sure the high is thrilling
But did you like that low? The crying, the shaking, the cool
ceramic floor on your cheek?
Do you know what withdrawals from a person feel like?
Did you forget the bitter taste of betrayal so soon?
Don't do this. Get it together! Keep that barrier up.
Don't. Let. Them. In."

†

Even what's rooted can pack up and run
Leave you feeling like you lost a limb.

A part of you.
And when you love them so hard your heart is already broken
while they're still here...
You're in for a bad one.
Or, you say, "maybe he's my forever"

†

I'm so afraid that this won't work out
I'm so afraid that it will.

25 THIS HOLY WAR

How can you worship me
And wound me
At the same time?
What do you really know of love
If you think condescension
Should have any room to grow
Inside of this city in the clouds?
Inside of my glimmering castle, where my pedestal resides

†

How do you adore me
And use me as a punching bag
As both a pawn and an enemy
In this holy war you've waged
But love shouldn't be a fight
And this battlefield shouldn't be littered
With our blood, sweat and tears

†

How do you keep me here
In a state of perpetual pain and fear
Shouldn't a union make us feel strong?
Shouldn't we be conquering together?

It doesn't matter anymore who is right and who is wrong
It never mattered
Because olive trees don't grow here
And all of the forgiveness has bled out of me

26 R.I.P. CHORD

Leave it to me to take something beautiful and burn it to the ground
Leave it to me to ruin a fun time
I couldn't take the pain
I couldn't make sense of this fate
So, leave it to me to pull the rip chord

†

Leave it to me to take us both down
Leave it to me to realize too late
I didn't know this would happen.
I didn't know I'd feel this way
So, I apologize for asking for too much
Leave it to me to drop this bomb that was too heavy for me anyway

†

Leave it to me to want what I can't have
Leave it to me to make you feel blue
You were good to me
You were good for me
So, leave it to me to cut and run before I fall any harder.

27 TANGLED UP IN YOU

I long to be back in your arms
If I knew that the last time would *be* the last time
I would have stayed there longer
I would have held you tighter
I would have tried to lock every millisecond into the memory
of every cell in my body.
I would have breathed you in one last time
I would have kissed you deeper
I would have gazed longer into your eyes
I would have told you I love you in a way that wraps around
you permanently and keeps you safe and warm for always
I would have cradled *your* dreams and the life *you* want in a
hammock of intent and I would have manifested it all for you
Because I'd do fucking anything to make you happy

†

Instead, all I manage to do is wreak havoc like a hurricane and
then survey the damage in shame and dismay.
The apologies will never be enough
I should have paused before spinning out about how this hurts
me
And taken a moment to appreciate that you deserve to live your
life on your terms.
I'll always hope that's what you are doing

28 XVI

Every step of the way, I knew this was coming
Razor sharp
Then a painful ache
Being sore days later
Remove this limb with the sharpest blade
The anesthetic wears off and I'm left in agony

†

Where did you go?
When did you go?
Did you know?
Did you run, and leave your shell to handle it?

†

Did you handle me?
The way you had always planned?
Break me as promised
Or keep the grenade from going off
Tie the tourniquet tight
Because nothing could erase that blood stain
If I fall apart right here right now

†

In love you give
You give your time

You give your heart
You give your limbs
I did.
You took.
You took everything I gave you like I was a child handing you a
rock I found
It might not be much
And it might not be enough
But it's all I have to give in the world

29 XVII

We met on a fault line
On the jagged edge of something delicate
The sharp corner of a single piece of paper
While it leave the harshest of stings, it can also crumple into a
ball or shred with ease

†

We were always destined to fall apart
It was a doomed mission
A reckless fairy tale
Two ships attempting to rendezvous in the night
Instead, we crashed headfirst into each other and sank

†

We were each others' keepers, though
You protected me and I protected you
The wind howled around us but the chill could never touch our
bones
When we had each other and the heat between us
When we could trace the delicate edges of each other
Instead of the balancing act on our slippery slope.
It was the vulnerability we exchanged
That demanded we risk it all
But it was only a matter of time our hearts became casualties.

30 XVIII

It tore me apart
To be stitched back together by you
You dragged me through, kicking and screaming
And I made it Hell for you
Then, I stood up, dusted myself off, and walked away
Stronger and sure of what is right for me

31 XIX

When you look up into the sky tonight do the stars spell out,
"I Miss You?"
Does the moon turn into a crying emoji?
Can you taste my need in the air?
I bet you'll find it there, in all the spots
Where you made love to me in the dark

†

Does it bother you now?
My unspoken words
My loud thoughts echoing as they reach you
Interrupting your day, seeking your attention
When I know you have more important things to do

†

"It is what it is," I say
Except I remember when it was what it was
And it breaks my heart in two.
Can I share it with you?
I want to be in your arms again

32 XX

You'll be OK because you gotta be
As for me, I can hardly breathe
You call our love a disaster
I choke on my tears
Emotions I can't master
Because, to me, it was beautiful

†

Heavy-handed and frozen-hearted
My moans rise up, lips parted
Trying to cover up this pain
Force a smile on my face
Laying in the tub, last of my dreams circling the drain
Maybe it's easier for you this way

†

But I'll be OK because I gotta be
These dreams of mine gotta come true eventually
And I'll figure them out in time
Make a life that's all mine
Forever wonder about the one who sipped what my soul is
made out of
And poured the cup out into the dirt
But it wasn't supposed to hurt.

33 XXI

Love saved me
And love destroyed me
And now I'll spend the rest of my life
Walking this Earth
Searching for anything like you
To breathe into my mouth again
To hold my fears and secrets
To cradle my face in hand
Wipe away the tears
To consume me and invigorate me
To merge into one
To look at me the way you did
To see me
Because nobody else can
I'm a ghost
But you haunt me

34 XXII

I feel like we never quite recovered from the last hotel night.
It was never the same again after that.
What we had was gone
I really tried
But I felt like a disappointment to you, daily
And I can't live like that
Constantly trying to earn back your love and affection
Always coming up short
That desperate shit isn't for me
It's not what Queens do
And I know you've only known me on my knees
But I assure you, who I've been is not who I am
And I'll never kneel or beg again

35 XXIII

I will never again let an entire parade of red flags
Pulling a shipping container of baggage
With hundreds of dancing double standards
A six hitch of graceful manipulations
A symphony of swan song

†

Make me feel like this.

†

It was a spectacular show
A marvelous display
But, honey, I'm over here twirling and sparkling
And you're a distraction.

36 XXIV

Your hand on my cheek
Your lips tasting my tears
Moving into me
Merging into one

†

Shared soul
Forever spring
The winter doesn't go
Here
Breathing life
Burning love
Head spinning like I'm drunk
Hot flush
Blood rush
Whisper in hush

†

Gripping flesh
Licking sweat
Teasing tongues
God, this is love
Passioned cries
Like sinful lullabies

†

Can't let you go
Wanting you to know
What's deep within
I'm there again
Reaching that high
Terrified of goodbye
Just say you'll try
Even if it's a lie

37 XXV

The greatest art we ever made
Was our love story
The masterpiece of my shaking body in the moonlight
Awake and alive
Spent but hungry for more
Always hungry for more from you

†

What once saved me has become another thing to heal from
You got me good.
Pulled me in
I knew you would.
I just wanted to belong to you
I only wanted everything

38 XXVI

Your hand in mine
Or mine in yours
Your smile for me
Holding me close

†

All the encouragement
Support and compliments
You told me to fight
And your hand was at my back
So I did

†

You made me strong enough to stand without you

†

Days and nights
Jokes and laughter
Intensity in our eyes got the blood pumping in our veins
White hot kisses under starry skies
You told me to do it for you
So, I did

†

Now the time has come

The end is here
We knew it would be
Walking away hoping you couldn't see me shaking
Just wanting to be back in my hero's arms again
But you made me strong enough to stand without you
So, I will

39 XXVII

I resent that you're the best thing in my life
Why am I such a fool for you?
When we aren't together and the fog lifts
I see you for what you are
And this for what it is
But, when I'm with you, I'm so caught up
So lost in this Haze
So swept away
Held hostage by my own feelings
I am tethered to you by a golden chain
And your touch lights me up inside
Your love invigorates my spirit
I'm buzzing with joy

†

Then you're gone again

40 XXVIII

Your harsh words pierce my eyes like thorns on a rose bush
Tears stream down my cheeks and I think they're made of blood.
No amount of time or soft touch will soothe this.

41 XXIX

You've carved your name into my heart
You might as well carve into my skin, too.
You've already squeezed the life out of my soul
So, squeeze the breathe out of my neck
We exist on a clock
The moving forces dancing around that truth
Like spinning teacups
Until one of us can't take it
And gets off this ride
Our names that I wrote in the sand are long gone now
But maybe somewhere there is a tree with our initials carved
into it
And maybe it'll bleed for you, too.

42 XXX

The days and nights I cried over you
The years where I wasn't enough
The loneliness that has consumed the better part of a decade
And now that I stopped catering to you
Stopped worshiping you
Stopped making everything in my life about you
Now you want to act like you are the victim
And you're so hurt
And you love me so much
Where was that love when you were stabbing me in the heart?
If things went back to the way they were
And I put you first again, and myself last—how you like—
How long before *you* would go back to the way you were?
How long before you would take up with other women again?
How long before you'd turn to them to trash me?
How many months would you lie to my face?
How many more years would I have to spend crying, wondering why I'll never be enough for you?
That's not me anymore.
I'm building a life I enjoy and I'm not letting you control and hurt me anymore.
I'll be the monster and the villain in your story
I really don't care; as long as I have peace

43 XXXI

I give until I break
You take until I drain
I jump through hoops
Walk on tightrope, dance through flames
Tame your tigers and juggle everything you throw at me
Just for you to keep coming up with ways I've failed to impress
you

†

You brag about being a liar and a manipulator
And I can't explain what I see in you
Because underneath the beautiful webs you've spun of pretty
words
There's a master of deceit, a cold-hearted killer, a cheating
husband.
You brought me new horizons and emotions and sensations I
only dreamed
But I can't trust you
I don't know what was real and what was a fabrication
Your twisted little games

44 XXXII

A part of me wants to come out the other side of this
But it feels like the light at the end of the tunnel is an oncoming train and
I welcome the impact

45 XXXIII

My desperate heart wants to reconcile your brutal plans with
your love spun words.
I want to find a connection somewhere in between.
A link to your two extremes
And what you told me you planned to do to my fragile mind
And my glass heart
I wish to find meaning in all of this
Something deeper than your need to hurt and wound
Some reassurance of your love
To soothe the pain and bruises
And lick away these tears
But all there is
Is this nagging *knowing*
This isn't right

46 XXXIV

You'll never get my softness or vulnerability again
That chapter is over
And the book is closed, burned in a fire

†

You probably don't even get that you had the best of me
You probably didn't even recognize that
Because all you wanted was destruction

†

But you don't know me that well
You don't know that I resurrect but I can also destroy
Tread carefully, or you'll find out

47 XXXV

I'm stained
And I'll never be clean
Pour a Merlot on a white rug
And you'll see what I mean

†

I've scrubbed, I've bleached
I've raged and I've cried
All of the people that swore they loved me
They lied

†

So, I'll let you down again
Because you lied, too
And I'll take your abuse
Because I hurt you

†

And we'll go on this way
Or one of us will break free
There's only one way this ends
Because it's the death of me.

48 XXXVI

You failed
You didn't break me
I'll glow brighter than the sun
And you'll still be you
Siphoning your power off your victims

49 XXXVII

I woke up from nightmares, all night long
Only to realize, every time, they were real
I can't escape you in my sleep
Thoughts of you haunt my waking mind, too
I wish I could erase you

50 XXXVIII

You don't believe in luck
But I don't believe there's an after you
I extend the deepest sympathies to past me
For what she endured all those years before you
Two months can feel like a lifetime
When you're seen for the first time

†

You are too good to be true
So, I search for the lies
I doubt you and I roll my eyes
And I cling to thoughts that I'll catch you in your deceit
And sometimes, when it hurts a little more than I can take
I hurt you
And I'm sorry

†

Sometimes I struggle with the words
I can't even speak to you
I can't say the things I want to say
You always know

51 XXXIX

I realize now that my existence is my afterlife
This is Hell
It's not real
And it is real
This suffering I feel
The joy and the love that gets ripped away from me
This is my punishment for awful deeds
That I don't remember
From another life
It's never going to end
This, too, shall *not* pass
There is no holding on until daylight comes
This all just *is*
And there is a sort of comfort here

52 XL

Every sign and red flag was smacking me in the face
And I saw them
But I made the choice to ignore them.
I watched the manipulation gymnastics
The crocodile tears
The bullshit spill from those lips
I knew what it was
But I existed in this fantasy you spun me
Because it felt fucking amazing

†

And now I feel like a fool
For feeling wounded
When I *knew* it was coming and I *knew* you were a fraud
I served you up my weaknesses, fears, and secrets
And you made a feast out of me
I'm too good for this
Why do I feel this way?

53 XLI

All I wanted was to be held.
I've been craving it for weeks
I didn't get quite enough the last time and was hoping for it to
be enough
But it crumbled in my hands and I'm left still needing
Your arms around me
My head on your chest
Your heartbeat in my ear
Telling me everything is OK and right and good
That I'm safe and loved
That I'm enough
That I matter

†

Now I have to live in the cold with my demons for company
And they don't hold me like you do

54 XLII

Mostly I'm thankful
For feeling alive again
I've come through the darkest of times
And these first gulps of fresh air filling my lungs
My heart beating with purpose
Knowing I'm going to be just fine
It's a new day
A new Era
I'm on top

55 XLIII

I'm relieved for this clarity
The realization that all the things I thought I needed to be happy
Everything I pinned my happiness to
That I thought I had to achieve
I don't really need it.
It was all so limiting to be striving for these things
Which, once I had them, I wouldn't have been happy, anyway
Now I can see that those big, lofty dreams
Weren't even what I wanted anymore
What I want is really much simpler than that
And it's everything that I already have.
I just needed to take those blinders off and see it.

56 XLIV

You are me
And I am you
On this ride
Sharing this remarkable human experience
We all feel so alone in feeling the same emotions
But what if we reached out
Across the divide
And took each other by the hand
Would we no longer feel so singular?

57 XLV

I wanted to scream, "I love you," as loud as it felt in my heart
Now, I want to scream, "I miss you"
But no amount of screaming ever brought anyone back
Not from the dead.
Not from the void.
Believe me, I've tried.

58 XLVI

I know you did me a favor letting me go
I know you're wrong for me
I know you're dangerous
I know this isn't real
I know I'm just hooked on this feeling.

†

You know what to say
You know what to do
You know how to touch
You know how to get to me
You know its true

†

Some fun just isn't worth having

59 XLVII

I feel my power because I know myself
I know what I am and what I bring
I know what I'm worth (priceless)
And what I deserve

†

So, no, I'm not going back
I don't regret it
But it won't happen again
Time for me to shine in a way I couldn't with you

60 XLVIII

My entire soul hurts
Please just get this out of me
This hurt, this sorrow, this rage, this madness
I can't breathe
I can't stop
I can't sleep
I can't eat
Everything inside of me feels wrong
Like a shattered mirror that was put back together
But all of the pieces are in the wrong spots

61 XLIX

I'll never be someone who pretends to be what I'm not
Never again will I allow myself to forget
That I'm a warrior
I won't act like I haven't been broken
Like I didn't fall to my bedroom floor sobbing just this morning
Like every day isn't a struggle
My head needs to be reminded frequently
About this strong, resilient heart beating in my chest
And since all I have is me
I'll be the one to do it.
Maybe I'll never find who I used to be again
Maybe she's really gone
I'll just pull this version of me back up
Because I'm pretty sure she's something special and deserves to be happy, too.

62 L

Somewhere on a side street
Between my fear and insecurity
My thoughts running wild
With my heart pounding underneath
My breath caught in my throat
And maybe it was just the cold
But, then, she reached for my hand
And a warmth began to grow
Between our two bodies
And the space between my head and heart
Her soft skin and her smiling lips
And the blush that spread across my cheeks
My smile must have been wide
I could feel it in my teeth

†

So, our foot steps matched
And our laughter danced
And the walk signal lit up
She led the way and guided me
And held open the door.
I thought "I could get used to this" and
"God this feels so right"
And somewhere along the way, I lost the fight or flight
Honey, I'm home

63 LI

I won't ever become hardened or cold
My heart will always be soft
Scar tissue won't grow here
I will always love
Because *I am love*
It radiates out of me
And sometimes it means I'll be hurt
People will treat me and my heart carelessly
They'll use their words cruelly
And take me for granted
But that's just a reflection of them.
That's who they are.
I am still love.
I will still love.

64 LII

Claws are out
Playtime is over
You want a fight I'll give you one
You thought I was easy Prey
But I'm about to make a meal out of you
I was down but I'll never be out
And you woke a sleeping Beast
So, I hope you learn to sleep with one eye open
I hope you brace for the attack
Because I'm not like you
I welcome a challenge
A true warrior doesn't target the weak

65 LIII

The worst thing I ever did
Was when I lost the will to fight
Succumbed to the misery and the pain
Gave in to the Nothing
I stopped caring about myself
And lost my survivor instincts
I can't ever let that happen again

66 LIV

I knew you were full of shit the entire time
And I resented you for it
Constant shakeup
Rooting down
But frantically looking for a way out
I clung to you helplessly
Knowing you were sucking the life from me
Desperate to be saved
By the fiend killing me

†

Now I'm free
And it's bittersweet
My joy is returning
There's a smile on my face again
But your lies felt so good

†

I want to erase all the bad in you
All the bad there was
And remember only the good
Was there any?

67 LV

You got your hooks in deep
But there are so many parts of me
That you were never able to touch
And will never have
You can gloat
Take your digs at me
Laugh it up
But I was there
I was there
I know the truth
You never had me
And you never will

68 LVI

I had to learn as a child that people who say they love you
Can and will hurt you
I've also learned that in this life
You will encounter people who will show you kindness beyond
your own comprehension
And you won't trust it
But it's real and they mean it

†

And there is a full spectrum in between
Of people who will hurt you and love you
In varying degrees.
Don't let the ones who hurt you harden you
Love anyway
Be kind anyway
Love is Hate's only enemy
Kindness is a formidable weapon against Cruelty
Even when it doesn't seem like it

69 LVII

Haunted by your memory
And the way you treated me
Burned into my heart and soul
And the guilt for allowing it
Now you spin your false narrative
As easily as you spun your lies to me
But I know what's true

70 YOU WHO GOT ME THROUGH

You speak of my strength like I'm someone that inspires
We talk for hours about everything under the sun—and the moon
Slowly it gets better
The fog lifts, my smile returns
I made it out and I'm still standing
But it was you who got me through

†

I showed up so raw
Nerves exposed, every breath was painful
You know pain, too, so you didn't look away
Your compassion was bigger than the ache inside
I could have done it on my own, eventually, painfully
But it was you who got me through

†

You held me in your arms
And you kissed my scars
Your eyes traveled through my soul and back again
We joined, as much as we could
And we laughed like people who have never cried

It doesn't feel so dark anymore, and I think I'll be OK
But it was you who got me through

71 LVIII

I would have continued loving your dark
As much as I loved your light
But when your dark began to seek me out
Like a missile, intent on destruction
I knew I could never stay
You pulled me down like quicksand
And the more I fought, the more you won
You broke my trust and my heart
You turned my already chaotic mind into a war zone
But the worst thing you ever did
Was turn me into a stranger to myself.
For that, I will never forgive you

72 LIX

I thought Love was a curse
The way it burrowed into me
Powerless to stop it
The agony left in its wake
My heart Haunted by what was,
What could have been and what will never be
Then, the raw ache fading into a tender bruise
And the fear of it happening again—
It always does

†

Now I see that Love isn't a curse
Love is a miracle
Love is Life
Love is unrestrained Joy
Love is birth
Love is union
Love is safety
Love is the most beautiful thing there is in the whole world

†

It's not Love that hurts;
It's the absence of it

73 LX

Sorry I won't change to be what you want
(Too much pride)
Sorry I put myself through this
(Days and nights I cried)
Sorry I forgot my worth
(And all the magic I have inside)
And I'm really, really
Sorry I ever fucking met you
There ain't enough I'm-sorries for this sorry excuse for a love
affair

†

I'm gonna be honest and say
I liked the way that smile on my face felt
And if it's quite OK
I'll say I miss that look that made me melt
But you lie like you breathe
And I can't have that on me
So you're out with the trash
Cos of all the times you made me feel like it

†

Guess I thought I could stay one step ahead of you
Like, I'll play your game but only if I win
Shoulda thought better cos I deserve better
Than to let someone mistreat me

I swear I'll never let it happen again

†

Walking on eggshells, blowing up landmines
Putting together the puzzle with all the times you lied
Not gonna do this. Matter of fact, screw this
Time to show myself the love I've been denied

†

Nothin' hurts worse than forgetting who I am
Learned my lesson about betraying my own heart
I swear I'll never, ever beg ever again
I couldn't go on like that
So, I picked myself up and I walked away

†

Used your red flags to tie me to the bed post
Crossed every line and boundary I had
I deserve a love both passionate and tender
Turns out my love's the best I've ever had

74 LXI

Your accusations are confessions
I read the lines of you
Like my own palm
You bare your fangs
And pretend it's a smile
Your love looks an awful lot like hate
And I'm filled with enough hatred for the both of us

75 LXII

Only place in the world I want to be is alone
In a very old bear's den.
A den older than me, maybe.
A den that has sheltered mama bears and their litters of cubs.
Kept them warm, dry and protected
from the harshness of the winter outside.
I'd want to barricade the entrance with brick and concrete
keeping everyone out and me in.
It's my softer side that calls it a "den," by the way
When really I want to say cave.
This is what I dream of most
While I wait for the nothing at the end.

76 LXIII

Why is it that we never see the knife coming
From the whispered promises?
That's always where it comes from.
That's who will tear your heart out

†

You could have just stabbed me in the heart.
You didn't have to remove the entire thing and take it with you

77 LXIV

I want to scream at the top of my lungs and punch and kick and flail and be inconsolable and unrestrainable and for the sight and sound of me to be unsettling and traumatizing to behold.

†

I want to go back and be frozen in a moment where my rage was more than I could bear silently, but it was understood, and so, it was allowed.

78 LXV

Watching the soft snowflakes fall from inside
my warm living room, in absolute silence
with a cup of tea in my hand, should be pleasant.
It should be calming.
It just makes me angrier.
All this rage in me with nowhere to go
and everything that has the audacity
to not be affected by it
while I'm being torn to shreds inside.
Fuck you, beautiful, picturesque snowflakes
and your stupid, peaceful moment.
I can't breathe.

79 LXVI

You speak to me in a language nobody else would understand
Directly to my soul
Your eyes to mine
You make me feel completely naked and on display
Because you can see right down to every part of me
It's terrifying and thrilling
Equal parts grounding me and I'm spinning
There's nowhere in the world I feel safer than in your arms

†

But you can also make me freeze and go mute
My mind blanks and I forget how speech works
I worry over you all the time
And I fear hurting you, and I fear losing you

80 LXVII

Of all the things you took from me
The moments were the very worst.
Moments of joy
Moments of laughter
Moments when all we had was each other
I guess memories can lie
And photos show deception and illusions

†

What I wanted it to be
What you wanted it to mean
The love we shared
And everything in between

†

When it all went down in flames
And everything we had was lost
The hardest part was losing myself
And wondering if I'll ever get me back

81 LXVIII

Nothing seems real anymore
It's all fuzzy
Like it's happening to someone else
But the hurt in my soul is more than sympathy pains
I feel like I've wasted my life
Unsure of how I'm supposed to start over
How to put one wobbly foot in front of the other
Everything in me just wants to hide
I'm not cut out for reinvention
I'm not cut out for war
I'm not cut out for love, or it's aftermath
I'm not cut out for any of this

82 LXIX

Nobody can hear me screaming
From inside this fishbowl
Where the water hasn't been changed in years
It's dark, I can't see
The only sounds I can hear are angry screams
And bitter curses
They weren't always coming from me
But now they are

†

Nobody has looked over at me in I don't know how long
Time stopped somewhere
Nobody notices. Nobody cares
The ache inside is constant
And so it's comfort
Who would I even be without it?

83 LXX

I picture you laying there
Looking up at the ceiling
Feeling lonely and empty inside
And I'm laying here
Doing the same damn thing
And wondering what this is all for

†

If I stop will you stop?
Can we take it all back?
I don't want to fight
I want this all to go away
But I can't back down if you're gonna take another swing
If you promise to stop, I'll stop

84 LXXI

After years of walking on eggshells, it looks like you detonated.
You took everything down with you.

†

What if I had left the first time?
To think of everything that wouldn't have happened
All of the trauma erased
All of the tears not shed
All of the lives unaffected
It's all my fault

†

I bring tragedy and chaos
You bring cruelty and devastation
We were a match made in Heaven, maybe
But you put me through such Hell

85 LXXII

It sickens me that even after everything
A part of me still has the impulse to run back to your arms
Give up everything
For more with you
Even knowing it was bad, and wrong.
Even knowing how low you think of me
Even after the terrible things you've done
A part of me wants to forgive you
A part of me wants to continue on
A part of me wants to erase the last several months
Cos maybe we could have made it work this time

86 LXXIII

Everything reminds me of you
I'm walking around like an overfilled water balloon
Liable to burst at any moment
Barely holding it together
All because you fell apart

†

I sleep in your bed with a pile of stuff beside me
So I feel less alone
And so I don't end up in the same spot I was
The last time you put your hands on my body
It doesn't really work

75 LXXIV

All alone
Ain't nothing new
Up all night with memories of you
And it grates my heart
Every single day I'm fallin' apart

†

Breaking free is supposed to be
Unshackled chains and possibilities
But I'm still boxed in
Stomach tight, can't breathe, cryin'

†

Can't trace back where it all went sideways
Wrinkles on our imagery
Like the ones on my face
Sunken in
Traveling back from now to then

†

Tears flowing out my eyes
Down to my lips
Taste them with my tongue
And remember your kiss
This isn't where I want to be

What is it you want from me?

†

All that was good just like Heaven
So desperate to find
What was real and what were games
Between you and I
Don't need one more shot to see
That you're no good for me

†

Breaking you like a habit
I don't need another fix
When I have him beside me
Showing me how it's supposed to be
How it never was with you and me
I'm not ever coming back now
I'm not leaving his arms
Trading fear of the unknown
For The Devil I Know
That ain't my story anymore
That was yesterday's war
And its a new day

88 LXXV

I wonder if you're sleeping
Or if your thoughts are laying with mine
I wonder just what it would take to end this
How much of the sacrifice would have to be mine
Like always

89 LXXVI

Nobody to trust
Not anybody
Nowhere to turn
Every face is a mask
With a monster underneath
Fake smiles with sharp fangs
Manipulation and knowing which buttons to push
Knowing how to twist the knife
Spilling blood so subtle
So discreet
You don't even know how much you've lost
Until you can't stand anymore
And the puddles been lapped up
And the knife was taken and wiped and tossed into a dumpster.
Was it the one you love?
Was it the one you hate?
Was it someone in between?
Was it a stranger
Who finally destroyed you?

90 LXXVII

I don't feel anything anymore
I know that should be a problem
That should bother me
I should want to change that
But it feels like freedom
To not be shackled by emotions
To not be dependent on how another treats me
To be able to just shrug my shoulders and walk away
I can do that now
I can leave you where I found you
I don't even care
I'll just go back to bed

91 LXXVIII

For years he made me feel like I wasn't good enough
Then I got out
I'm not about to let anyone else treat me the same way.
If you have a problem with me
With the way I look
With the way I live
With the way I handle my problems
There's the fucking door.

92 LXXIX

My heart is just too heavy for you to hold
I'm sorry it comes out in random downpours
of poison hail.
I'm sorry the hurt seeps out of me like an oil spill
Over everything precious and good about you.
I'm sorry so much of it has been filled
with so many layers of cement
that I can't even make any sense of you
and your loving, sentimental heart.
I'll never be good enough for you
and you're always going to want and deserve more.
I try to show you I love you
But I do a piss poor job, and it's clear
That what it would take is a whole skill set I've never had.

†

My heart's been broken so long I think it set this way
Like a broken bone
Phantom limbs evoking memories of what was
Scar tissue and keloids growing over
all the cracks and broken pieces
Never again to be the soft
The pink
The tender
The hopeful
Ravaged and destroyed and barely beating at all

93 LXXX

I want my childhood back
I want my trust back
I want all of the love back that I poured into you
I want my nerve back
And my voice
I want to know what to believe
And to wade through all of the bullshit
And never fall again

†

After everything you've done to me
What I hate most about you
Is that you're not here
None of this is real
None of it's real
I want to wake up from this nightmare now

94 LXXXI

Did you forget I'm a Lioness?
While you proceed without caution
Like there aren't consequences
Like I'll lie down and submit
With claws so sharp and teeth so strong
Survival my drive
Protecting what's mine, in my veins
Did I forget that I'm a Lioness?

95 LXXXII

It's raining here, in my room
I can't see through the fog
Of my glassy eyed misery
Drowning in this salty flood
And praying desperately for you to save me
But you won't come
I've never been more alone in my life

✝

Its dark now, here
And bitter cold
I'm shaking and I'm sweating
My sobs cut my throat
Like a thousand betrayals by you
Pain ripping through me
Penance for everything I've done wrong
Every way I've fucked up
And the consequences of my choices

✝

Bleeding out and throwing up
Clutching my rosary beads in my right hand
Fist to my chest
The other on my belly
Repeating Hail Marys and Our Fathers
Like He will have mercy on me now

It's too late
To beg forgiveness of a God I don't believe in
But I'll do anything...anything

†

The rest of my life awaits
The torture has ended
The rain has stopped
The darkness, no more
But in my heart the storm lingers
In my soul the memories cannot ever be washed away
The agony never fades
Forever I will be crushed
For my lifetime I will grieve
And it still won't be enough

96 LXXXIII

I don't need you.
I want you.
I won't die without you
But if I do die
You'd be what I miss about living
You aren't air
You aren't water
But God damn, you are a fire inside me
And those burning flames make me feel alive

97 LXXXIV

I want to look like an angel when I drag you through Hell
Someday you might hate me
But you'll always love me more

98 LXXXV

She tore through me like wildfire
Nothing would stop her until she was ready
I would suffer for trying
My blood, sweat, and tears
Soaked into my bed
Branded onto my memory
Daring to think I knew better than destiny
Cosmic fate's plans unraveling at my insistence
Not now. I want this, but not now.
What happens next is a mystery
that haunts my darkest thoughts and fears
It's all my fault

99 LXXXVI

I'm so afraid of what else survival mode will cost me
The deeper in love with you I fall, the more terrified I am.
It's just that I've never had it like this
And now that I do, it's a hell of a thing to lose
Because as much as I don't think my heart could withstand it,
Even more than that, I worry for yours

†

And whose arms will comfort you?
Who's lips will join yours?
Who will take care of you?
Who will bring a smile to that handsome face?
And melt over the way that smile reaches your eyes
Like you light up from within?
I think the light in me may be burned out forever
But making you smile will suffice

†

The rest of our lives just isn't enough
And any less than that would be devastating.
I can't do this without you
And I can't stand seeing what we had burn out, too
How many setbacks does it take to kill a relationship?
Will we ever get our fairy tale?
Our Christmas morning?
Our farmhouse sunsets

And echoes of laughter and little feet running?

†

The life we never got to have flashes before my eyes
When I'm awake. When I'm asleep.
I'm Haunted by things I spent my whole life not knowing I
wanted
Until you
Until we created life together
Now I'm unraveling inside while the shell of me moves in
silence
And smiles
And lies
And pretends
It takes everything in me to make everything OK for everyone
else.

100 LXXXVII

Your lips on my neck
And your hands on my hips
My insides burn up
And my fingers try desperately to get you closer,
as close as can be
When you kiss me I become lava
Your touch takes me out of my head and out of my body
But I feel everything

†

There is no deep enough
I want you all the way inside me
There is no closer
That two people can be
My soul and yours are the same
The two halves want to be together and made whole again

101 LXXXVIII

You deserve better than picking up the shattered pieces he left
You love me like I'm the whole moon
A Super Blue Blood Moon
When I feel like a broken, empty shell
You make me feel like a precious and rare jewel
Like I matter
Like I'm not a waste of space and time
When you hold me I don't feel so cold and desolate
You fill me with a love and a hope I've never known
I wish you got the best version of me
But you make me want to be that

102 LXXXIX

So, what do I do with these feelings?
Where should I put all this sadness and regret?
All the longing and hope?
Just shove it away somewhere and pretend it doesn't exist?
Is that what you're going to do?
Or were you lying the entire time?

103 XC

Reality and fantasy
And the ghosts of the in-between
Prolonging the inevitable
Because the hint of needs being met in the moment
Is all I can get
But its not real
And I can't pretend for long
And neither can you
Then we are back to square one
with reality slapping us in the face
I'm terrified of the part where this ends

104 XCI

I want to stay
And I want to hear you say
Everything I need to hear
To take away every fear
I need to feel safe with you
But I need your words to be true
Don't just say it for me
If it's a God damn well-intentioned fallacy
I need guidance and protection
Your love and support feels like heaven
Reining me in with the discipline I never got
You think it's controlling, but I swear that it's not
To be loved so completely with the instinct to protect
Don't listen to these people and their desire to dissect
The relationships of others instead of focusing on their own
You and I can build whatever life we want
I want this to work because it's my dreams and my waking life
that you haunt
I want to trust you to lead
Your voice, eyes, and touch fill me with need
I know it's not you
And I'm sorry to ask for something untrue
Just kind of hoping it could take root
And you'd see the benefit and start to enjoy it, too
I fear that I disgust you, and you don't understand
How I can need you with everything I am
But you make me feel safe to have these needs met

You've done things for me I won't ever forget
If you walk away now I won't hold a grudge
I understand, it's not for you, but my feelings won't budge.
I just wanted this to work and I'm sorry I'm not what you're wanting
The idea of finding what I have with you anywhere else is so daunting
Because there's love and there's trust in this Heaven and Hell
Nobody on Earth could love me so well
But what good is it if I keep fucking up
Without any rhyme, rules or reason
No self love in my cup
But you bring me closer than I've ever been
Make me feel like I'm worth it
You're a God among men.
So, I just want to show you how rare and special you are
Make You understand how much I need you
Believe we'll go far
If we just hang on we can figure this all out
But I understand if you don't want to
And feel it's impossible
If I'm just too difficult
And not worth the trouble
If the love you give me
You don't get in return
No matter how hard I try
I have so much to learn

†

But you've changed my life
And you've set me free
Made me want to be your wife
You were the key
To whatever happens next
For you and for me
I don't have any answers
So my instinct is to flee
But just know it's not what I want
I want your arms and your love and protection
I want the only hurt I feel to come from you
I want to know in my heart no one else will ever cross me
Because I fell for such lies before
So take me, carry me, do whatever it takes
Make me listen
You're the only one who can.

105 XCII

I need that black and blue lovin'
And yours is gold and white.
I need to feel everything and nothing at all
Be out of my head tonight

†

I love you but it hurts too much
Sink or swim, fright or flight
In pain I can't measure
Just want to be out of my head tonight

†

Passion roaring through us both
Moaning and writhing under the moonlight
My fingers and lips on you
Going out of my mind tonight

106 XCIII

I want a bubble, or a cocoon around me
Around us
I want the whole world shut out
And only what matters inside
I want safety and security and stability
I want to know that when the fear creeps in
Or the hurt. Or the anger.
When I lash out or try to run
I want the one I share my space with to be able to stop me
Make me pause
Don't let me run
Don't let me fuck this all up
You're the only one who can
And it would only take a second
A few words
The desire on your part to take charge and fucking *lead*
And your unwillingness to makes me feel more unstable
More unsafe
More insecure
In this little nest
So, it makes me think you aren't the right person
to live in here with me

107 XCIV

Fourteen years today.
Fourteen years
Look at what it was all reduced to
All the love. All the joy. All the memories.
All the pain. All the anger. All the bitterness.
From where it all began
To today
Everything in between
Love, promises, a family
Torn apart and kicked through the dirt
Trust shattered. Betrayal. Hatred and rage.
Guess it's true what they say
About love and hate being two sides of the same coin.

108 XCV

Can't be loved for who I am
Can't be loved when I'm not
There isn't a version of me worth loving to be found
anywhere in this world
So, I guess it's time to go
Reaching for that old rip chord again.
Tonight is for drinking, music, and tears
And hoping the next embrace will glue me back together
into something that somewhat resembles a person.

109 XCVI

Spring will come and things will bloom
The cold and darkness will fade
Into New life
Maybe somehow, somewhere in the midst of it all
I'll find me again
Or be born anew.
And maybe someday, I'll smile again
And it'll be real
And I'll feel it from within

110 XCVII

To be young and in love is exquisite
The rush is a drug that cannot be bought
A high like no other
An experienced heart proceeds with caution
Taking out their fears and traumas from past lovers onto new
But you can't be fully immersed in love with one foot out the
door

†

To be old and in love is something sacred
To feel safe in another's arms
And at home in their presence
To build together and create memories and overcome obstacles
And come out stronger for it
I think that's why it's now and not then
To give us that feeling of relief
Like making our way home after a long, hellish journey
The way our hearts and souls have always known each other
Like conjoined twins separated at birth and raised apart
And now we found each other.
We won't have to do this alone anymore
Our souls have always known
It's our brains that needed to get it together
And I'll happily spend the rest of our lives keeping it together
Because I was never lucky until you told me you love me

J.M. MARIE

111 XCVIII

This damn heart of mine has been so beat up
Clawed, torn apart
Scorched and frozen solid
Then thawed and burned again
It shouldn't still work anymore
It doesn't make sense how it bends to your movements
And follows you anywhere
How it wraps around you in the dark and purrs.
It shouldn't be so willing to risk it all again
Pain, dismemberment, scars; permanent reminders
Just for a chance that the spark you lit inside doesn't go out
And maybe you'll stay
Maybe this will be forever

112 XCIX

The love in my heart is a red hot dagger
Melting it from the inside out in it's entirety
"Love" from another's lips is most certainly a lie
A fairy tale I don't believe in
Because it brings me dreams that wake me and ache me
A folksong I don't want to sing anymore
Because it burns my throat and makes my sad eyes leak
The only embrace I dare to trust
is the embrace of darkness and solitude
All I can count on is that the sun rises, and then it sets.

113 C

It's OK.
I'll just take every fear, every insecurity
all the things that terrorize my heart and mind constantly.
I'll take them and I'll fold them up.
Teeny tiny.
Into a little origami star
Then I'll swallow it and nobody will ever have to see it again.
Sorry I let some leak out for a second there
I'll get that shit under control

114 CI

I'll miss watching you sleeping
And wondering what you're dreaming
I'll miss your breath on my skin
And your arms pulling me in
The way we would slip into each other
Again and again and again
I'll miss your sparkling eyes
The way your lashes rested on your cheeks
And the tiny creases in the corners when you smile

115 CII

She says I'm like gazing into a bottomless wading pool
Her hands on my body telling a story with an artist's touch
She looks into my eyes and sees an entire universe
But they are just marbles of broken glass and playground sand

116 CIII

Everywhere you've ever touched me is scorched Earth
Raw, blistered, painful
I ache for your flames to lick my skin
again and again and again
It's the absence of your inferno that hurts;
Not being engulfed by you

117 CIV

Tides won't stop turning
Just cos your love stopped burning for me

†

Someday I might wish you well
Instead of telling you to go to hell
Everytime we speak

118 WEIGHTLESS

Feel nothing inside
Empty and light
And there'll be nothing left of me
When the ground is dirt cold
And bugs pick at my bones
There'll be nothing left of me

†

No hunger or thirst
Could ever feel worse
Than slipping in and out of dreams
The fog inside my brain
Can't tell if you're leaving or staying
Babe, there will be nothing left of me

†

So, go if you must
Guess I have to just trust
That it's quieter somehow, softer somehow
When there's nothing left of me.

119 CV

There was love in that house
Beneath the wails of a broken heart
Buried under the floor where your knee dug into my back
Hidden so securely, I couldn't see it
When the bruises scattered my skin
Maybe it was trapped inside the walls
your fists punched holes in
Or the door you broke
Maybe our sweet love still lives there
Pacing the living room, climbing the stairs
Waiting for you to return to the man you used to be
But the woman I am today will never forgive you
There was love in that house that we watched burn to the ground

120 CVI

You said my life would get better without you in it
You were so right
I didn't want to believe you.
I loved you so much
I miss you—and that part hurts.
It's hard to have things I want to tell you about, every day.
But there's no denying all the good things pouring into my life
now
And the weight that lifted when I stopped feeling so horrible
about myself
You became someone I didn't want to know.
Someone who uses insults and cruel words *just* to hurt
Someone who would crumble up the drawing
of a child that loves you
Just to show you never cared
Yes, I am certainly better off without you
And someday I won't miss you anymore
And someday I won't want to tell you about my day anymore
And someday I just won't think about you at all.

121 CVII

Prettiest thing I've ever seen
Dew drop on a bean
Sunlight shining in
Golden glow on your freckled skin
Our wild eyes hungry and free
All of me for you and all of you for me

†

Pleasure ripping through the seams
Sharing our impossible dreams
But Nothing's impossible for us who've seen
Glisten on a dew drop on a little pink bean

122 CVIII

When I drop to my knees they wonder why a Goddess would kneel
But I would get on my hands and knees and crawl to you
I'd get down to my belly and drag myself across gravel to you
That's just what my devotion looks like.
Absolute surrender and sacrifice
I don't hang my pride on the door
My pride is in the lengths I'll go for you
And get back up every time to do it again

123 WHEN YOU CALL AGAIN

I don't have anything left to give you
You've exhausted my mind
You've ravaged my body
You've laid waste to my heart
I will not let you have my soul
No, you cannot have my soul

†

You starved me
Had me on my knees begging for you
You skinned me alive
You set fire to my bones
So, no, you cannot have my soul
I will not let you have my soul

†

You can talk to my heart
Whisper any last words you just have to say
Satisfy your need to have the last word
Erase any doubt left in my mind that Goodbye is best
It will not change a thing
You still can't have my soul

†

I will not let you hurt me anymore

124 CIX

Out of all of the places
Throughout space and time
There was you and there was me
In the same place
At the same time
And I loved you without conditions
Beyond all reason
And I loved you with all of me and more
Expanding to accommodate this love that only ever grew
There was me and there was you
And now its an empty, dark room, gathering dust
Every so often a slight breeze coming in through the window
And my whisper on the wind
"I love you, Baby"

125 CX

So, were you just bored and decided you weren't done ruining me?
There were still some parts of me not bleeding
So, you just had to drag your claws through them
I crave you still.
I have spent the last few hours wishing I was in your arms.
Even knowing it was all lies...it was so real to me

126 CXI

I loathe and detest everything about myself
Everything on the outside and everything within
Every part of me, every inch of skin
Every piece and every cell
Trapped within this wretched Hell

†

This faulty brain and this tormented soul
Nothing good in me
Nothing I can see
Just pain so deep
I can't sleep

†

Liars and thieves to use and steal
Leaving me with nothing
But the hurt that won't heal
Endless war waged in this shell I inhabit
Just take what you want, you can have it

127 CXII

The tiny little portions I live on
Tiny little plate without a knife
To occupy the tiniest little space
Be as nonexistent as I can
A tiny little problem requires no solution
Bother you as little as possible
I'd ask you for the truth
What I really want to know
But you'll just say what you think I want to hear
So, I'd rather dream my medicated dreams
And be a hero, be special, be needed and desired
Until I have to wake up and be insignificant again

128 CXIII

The sands of time in my eyes burn, I'm blind
Watching the shores turn in yours
Sadness like never before
I'd turn it all around
Rip the foundation, new development
But I can't

†

I'm bleeding now and you're crying, asking how
I can't make you understand
And I don't expect you to stay
Just turn around
Keep walking, fade into the distance
I'm gone

129 CXIV

I creep through the dead of night
I hurt for the millionth time
I pray it will all be alright
But that's someone else's tale, not mine

†

My secrets lay at the grave of your hands
You haunt me just the same
I trusted you and you betrayed our plans
Still my heart jumps at your name

†

Never wanted to be made such a fool
I feel both useless and used
Nothing hurts as delicious as you do
I guess that's why you're my muse.

130 CXV

It hurts to hear the truth
When you believed the lie so long,
"I don't love you,"
Hits like a bullet when you thought it was as unconditional as
yours
Somehow I pulled a trigger of the gun you were holding
Must have been something in the chamber
Because I thought you'd always have the clip empty for me
So, I'll howl my hurt to the moon now
The rain on my face, mixing with my tears
Cooling my skin
Cleansing my wounds
The moon, like a womb
The moon cradles me tonight
I'm not alone under her divine light

131 CXVI

I won't suffer sweetly
My screams will rise into the atmosphere
My blood will soak the soil
I won't bear the weight of this with a smile
Or a humble shoulder shrug
I won't kneel quietly
Wait for it to pass
Grit my teeth and close my eyes, no
I will bite and I will claw and I will kick
You'll feel this agony too
You won't suffer bravely
You'll break long before I do

132 CXVII

A rage the likes of which you've never seen
It'll shake you to your core
It'll knock you off your feet
You don't know what to do with this
I've never been able to figure it out, either
My pain doesn't understand subtlety
And it sure as shit doesn't care about being polite

133 CXVIII

Pour the gas
Strike the match
Light of flame
Watch it all burn down.
You ever want to go somewhere so isolated
nobody could ever hear you,
And just scream until you can't make sounds anymore,
then bash your head into large rocks until you pass out?
Oh...me neither.

†

I dream of disappearing without a trace
and nobody ever finding me, alive or dead.
But my family would worry and be sad,
so, I don't.
Just keep wanting.

134 CXIX

I've been asking the question my whole life
And even when I get a satisfactory answer in the moment
It comes back
Haunting me
Begging me
Consuming my thoughts at times
Demanding to know
What
Is
It
All
For?

135 FIRES

I don't know why I set fires everywhere
As if I'm not an element of the Earth
I belong to the darkness
But even dark needs light.

†

Every scar has a story and you know all of mine.

136 CXX

You haunt my heart
And invade my nightmares
Grip the parts of me inside
That yearn and ache for you
And you drag them to your smiling lips
And take a bite
You mock me every minute
You wound me every second
And the longer I am apart from you
The more agony I am in
Pain, with or without you

137 CXXI

Life is an ugly, beautiful thing
full of twists and turns
that'll make you sick and exhilarated
and raise you to your feet after bringing you to your knees.

†

And maybe I'll forever regret the path I don't take,
but I've bent enough.
I've bent enough and I want to stand up straight.

138 CXXII

When it was over and my body gave out, I waited
I waited for the white light
Or to feel the flames on my skin.
Nothing but darkness
And immeasurable time
Then I couldn't feel you anymore
And I knew then that I was already in Hell.

139 LUNG LOST

You have me
Breathless and dizzy
Destroyed and reborn
Swept off my feet and crumbling to my knees
You have me
Gasping and choking
Sobbing and laughing
Reaching out for you and recoiling in agony
You have me
Blindsided and Lung Lost
Infatuated and Spinal Tapped
Obsessed and Brain Hemorrhaged
Life support, but you have me.

140 CXXIII

Alternating cries for help and screams for mercy
Until my voice is hoarse
My nails broken from clawing at the walls trying to get out
All the posts saying, "just reach out if you're struggling"
"I'm here for anyone who needs help"
"Mental health awareness"
All so full of shit its infuriating
But I'm too exhausted for fury
I'm too sad to keep trying
So, I die slowly

141 CXXIV

Watching my dreams slip further away
Is worse than a nightmare
I'm never going to be anything.
I'm a natural disaster

142 CXXV

What if we all wore our traumas and tragedies on the outside?
Scarred, burned, twisted, ugly
There wouldn't be a pretty face among us I think
Nobody unmarred
Nobody smooth and untouched by pain
By longing, by unmet needs, by violence
By loneliness or rage, by hopelessness and heartbreak
We would all just be creeping the planet with the goal of survival
Only our most Primal instincts
Nothing else would be necessary or particularly interesting
I think I could know a little bit of Peace there

143 CXXVI

He said
when I'm begging him to stop abusing me
that I sound like a scared, desperate animal
that's been cornered or trapped under the bed.
Like the sound of my voice,
in agony from his brutal and cruel words,
is annoying to him.
My pleas didn't reach the compassion hidden away
inside his heart.
It only drew his disdain.

144 CXXVII

Falling back into the dark arms that hold me
like a prison and a cocoon.
My eyes close and I'll hold my breath forever it seems.
Let it wash over me and pull me far from here.
I don't fear it anymore.
It's home.

145 CXXVIII

I'm not a survivor.
I live on life support.
I live out of fear, not desire.
Whoever I was going to be was stolen from me
The old me is a stranger
And whoever is living in my shell is someone I hate.
I can't be the things I need to be
For the people that I love
And the guilt is the heaviest thing I've ever carried
I'm looking out a window into my life
So detached and disturbed sometimes I can't even move.
But I go somewhere. I'm always going somewhere

146 CXXIX

If I could be better for you I would.
If I could glue together all these broken pieces
And become someone worthy of standing next to you
If I could feed your soul
And pour water into your garden
If I could hold you in the darkness
And spin with you in the golden light of new tomorrows
If I could promise you
If I could move in you like you move in me
If I could, I would. I swear.
If you put your blood in a locket for me
I'd wear you everywhere

147 CXXX

Love is exquisite in its agony
It's desperate in its hope
It's blinding, it's bright
Love is joyful in its honest yearnings
And its cravings for more
It grows from our bones
Giving us a reason
Giving us a promise
Giving us the feeling
That we are enough.

148 CXXXI

I want to be clung to so tight, all night long
I want there to be no space between us
For anything but the need and love to grow
I want our sweat to blend
Until there is no more "you" and "me"
Just one feral creature known as "we"
That would Wail in the night
And destroy villages if we were apart

†

I don't need you on one knee
I don't need promises you can't keep
Tonight's enough
Let's leave marks that won't ever fade
Allow passion and pleasure to rule us
You don't ever have to fear me
And I refuse to fear what my body is craving
Just let me melt into you

149 CXXXII

I'm thankful for the breath in my lungs.
Though it is labored, I'm still here.
I'm thankful for my vision
and that when I woke up this morning
and opened my eyes, I could see.
I'm thankful for the roof over my head,
and all of my beautiful clothes, shoes and accessories
that I enjoy wearing.
I'm thankful to have food to eat.
Though I struggle with food, and with my weight,
and it more often than not makes me feel sick.
I am blessed to have it
when so many are hungry and going without.
I'm thankful to have people that care about me,
and people that I care about.
Love is the most precious treasure in existence.
Love is also an action.
To Love is the greatest thing you can do
with your short time on this Earth
and any opportunity you have to do it you'd be wise to seize it.
I'm thankful that I still love with my whole heart
even after the pain and suffering I've endured.
I hope that I always will.
I'm thankful for the beauty in nature.
From sunrises and sunsets to autumn leaves.
From waves meeting the sandy shores
to snow capped mountains.

Even in its death and savagery,
nature and this Earth are beautiful.
I'm thankful for music, poetry, books, art.
I'm thankful for the ability to express myself
and to experience the expression of others.
I'm thankful for the journey.
For the lessons.
May it lead to wholeness and peace.
Most of all, I am thankful for my children.
They have taught me more than I will ever be able to teach
them.
This life and this world wouldn't be the same without them.
I would do it all again, exactly the same.

ACKNOWLEDGEMENTS

I wouldn't be where I am now without the support and love of my family. Generational trauma is a curse, and it tears families apart. Mine consists of a lot of very strong individuals, and the love that we have for each other is unshakable. When people are willing to look deep inside at all the painful parts, then decide to break the cycle for the children, healing can happen. I am so glad that members of my family are strong enough to want to do this. I'm proud of you.

†

My children are my greatest source of pride and joy. They are my life's purpose. They are my favorite people. I am blessed to be their mother and I don't ever take it for granted. Thank you both for being mine.

†

To my dear friend River; We met when we were children, and we've figured a lot out along the way. I'm so impressed by you. Your compassion, your intelligence, your talent and the beauty that shines from within. I am so honored that you worked on this with me and I feel so lucky to have you in my life. I couldn't have done this without your help and your support. Your encouragement kept me going. You see my vision and what I'm trying to do here and you believe in it too. That means everything to me. Thank you for being my friend and my editor.

†

To Michael, who wiped countless tears and held me for hours on end. He, who brought laughter back to my heart, who provided a safe haven, and listened without judgment. Your big, open heart and compassion bring healing to the world. I love you and Thank you.

†

And for everyone who's ever been at their breaking point and fell to their knees but somehow found themselves rising, one shaky foot at a time. You inspire me.

RESOURCES

Here are some resources for anyone who may find them helpful. I'd rather you have them and not need them than need them and not have them. Please, don't be afraid to reach out. There is no shame in needing support!

†

National Suicide Prevention Lifeline
1-800-277-8255 or call/Text 988

†

Psychologytoday.com
For help finding a mental health professional in your area.

†

RAINN National Sexual Assault Hotline
1-800-656-HOPE (4673)

†

National Domestic Violence Hotline
1-800-799-7233
thehotline.org

†

SAMHSA (For substance abuse help)
1-800-662-HELP (4357)

samhsa.gov

†

Nationaleatingdisorders.org
For help with eating disorders

†

I meant what I said before; You can reach out to me anytime on Facebook or Instagram!
Be well, and I love you!

About the Author

J.M. Marie has lived in New England all her life. She is a mother of 2 humans and 1 ragdoll cat. Marie enjoys art, music and nature. She has had a love of reading since childhood and began writing early on, particularly poetry and fiction. J.M. has a fascination with the complexities of relationships and family dynamics. She loves to explore why people make the choices they make.

She has a passion for helping others. This is her first published book and she hopes to continue to share her writing.